Transportation

Motorcycles

by Mari Schuh

CAPSTONE PRESS
a capstone imprint

Little Pebble is published by Capstone Press,
1710 Roe Crest Drive, North Mankato, Minnesota 56003
www.mycapstone.com

Library of Congress Cataloging-in-Publication Data
Library of Congress Cataloging-in-Publication data is available on the Library of Congress website.
ISBN: 978-1-5157-7303-0 (hardcover)
ISBN: 978-1-5157-7309-2 (paperback)
ISBN: 978-1-5157-7315-3 (eBook PDF)

Summary: Provides an overview of motorcycles, including their features and the types of motorcycles.

Editorial Credits
Carrie Braulick Sheely, editor; Lori Bye, designer; Wanda Winch, media researcher;
Katy LaVigne, production specialist

Photo Credits
Alamy Stock Photo: Darren Kirk, 7, imageBROKER, 9, Michael Doolittle, 21 (all); Dreamstime: Papabear, 13; iStockphoto: ewg3D, 15, RapidEye, 11; Shutterstock: Anatoliy Lukich, 17, Andrey Armyagov, 8, Giovanni Cancemi, cover, Marcel Jancovic, 19, Philip Lange, 5, T. Sumaetho, zoom motion design

Printed and bound in China.
010429F17

Table of Contents

Fast Rides

A motorcycle speeds away.

See it go!

Parts

Start up the engine.

The engine makes power.

It makes a motorcycle move.

engine

Riders steer.

They use the handlebars.

handlebars

A rider twists the throttle.

He speeds up.

Zoom!

throttle

Look ahead!

The road curves.

A rider uses the brakes.

He slows down.

Kinds

Touring motorcycles

go on long trips.

Big tanks hold lots of gas.

gas tank

Superbikes go very fast.

Riders lean in.

Dirt bikes race on dirt tracks.

They have bumpy tires.

Some riders add parts.

They make changes.

Which one do you like?

Glossary

brake—a tool that slows down or stops a vehicle

engine—a machine that makes the power needed to move something

handlebars—the part of a motorcycle that the driver holds on to and uses to steer

steer—to move in a certain direction

throttle—a lever or handle that controls the speed of an engine

Read More

Dinmont, Kerry. *Motorcycles on the Go.* Minneapolis: Lerner Publications, 2017.

Morey, Allan. *Motorcycles.* Machines at Work. Minneapolis: Bullfrog Books, 2015.

Omoth, Tyler. *Building a Motorcycle.* See How It's Made. Mankato, Minn.: Capstone, 2014.

Internet Sites

Use FactHound to find Internet sites related to this book.

Visit *www.facthound.com*

Just type in 9781515773030 and go.

Super-cool stuff!

Check out projects, games and lots more at
www.capstonekids.com

Critical Thinking Questions

1. How do riders make motorcycles speed up and slow down?

2. Look at the photos on page 21. Name a way that some motorcycles can be different from one another.

3. How are motorcycles different from bicycles? How are motorcycles like bicycles?

Index